When My Grandma Died

When My Grandma Died

by Hollie J. Harbaugh
and Roger F. Miller

Illustrated by Charles Morris

CBP Press
St. Louis, Missouri

CBP Press
Box 179
St. Louis, MO 63166

Library of Congress Cataloging-in-Publication Data

Harbaugh, Hollie J.
When My Grandma Died.

Summary: Nine-year-old Abigail tries to come to terms with her grandmother's illness and death.
(1. Death—Fiction. 2. Grief—Fiction. 3. Grandmothers—Fiction)
I. Miller, Roger F. 1950-
II. Title.
PZ7.H2115Wh 1986 (Fic) 86-6800

ISBN 0-8272-4218-2

Printed in the United States of America

A Note to Parents

This is a very sad story about the death of a young girl's grandma. It is also a necessary story. How nice it would be if we could shield our children from all the pain and hurt that the world foists upon us. Unfortunately, this is not possible. What we can do is prepare our children for the hurting times, such as when a loved one dies. We can do this in a loving and simple way by letting them learn about what is involved in the process of death and burial.

When children lose a loved one, they experience many emotions, none of them pleasant. There is fear of the unknown, as circumstances around them change rapidly. Often, there is anger directed at God, parents, themselves, the deceased, or all of these.

We adults still struggle with the same kinds of issues. One of the ways we may cope with the dilemma of death is through denial. Denial seeks to assure us that if we can ignore the whole thing, it will go away and we will not have to confront it again.

The truth is, death will *not* go away. At some time in his or her life, everyone must confront grief and mourning. Children as well as adults must be taught to cope with these events in order to move more quickly and easily from disbelief and despair to hope and affirmation that life goes on, and that it can still be good.

Many people feel that, as a matter of course, children should be excluded from the funeral and all of its attendant activities. The best response we've seen to this sentiment is given by Rabbi Earl A. Grollman, long noted as an expert in the experience of grief:

> Death is sad, but sadness is an integral part of the life process. The funeral is an important occasion in the life of the family. The youngster should have the same privilege as any other member of his household to express his own love and devotion. To deprive him of a sense of belonging could well impair his future mental health.

> Explain in advance of the funeral the details of the service. The child will be more relaxed and less disturbed if he first understands what he will soon witness. All the emotional reactions that a child is likely to experience—sorrow and loneliness, anger and rejection, denial and guilt—can be considerably lessened if the youngster knows what is occurring and that adults are not trying to hide things from him.*

It is in this spirit that we offer you this book. We do not set out to scare your children. Rather, we have tried to provide you a resource with which you and your children, together, may explore the meaning of death as a part of life.

We suggest that you read this book first. Then give it to your children with the intention of sitting down with them and talking about the story, answering any questions they may have.

Abigail is a fictional character, but the emotions she experiences in the story are real. They are based on the reactions we observed in our own children when they experienced the pain of losing their grandparents to death. These are the feelings and questions of children we have observed in dozens of other funeral situations. These reactions could be your children's too. We hope this book will make that painful time a little easier.

Hollie J. Harbaugh
Roger F. Miller

*Earl A. Grollman, *Concerning Death: A Practical Guide for the Living*. Beacon Press, 1974, pp. 72-73.

This book is dedicated to the memory of grandparents everywhere, but especially to:

Mrs. Elma J. Harbaugh
Rev. Robert Karl Miller
Mr. Harold R. Watson

And also to our children:

Sarah and Seth Miller
Shelley and Kelley Harbaugh

They made us acutely aware of their loss and, in turn, inspired us to write this book.

When My Grandma Died

My name is Abigail. People who know me well call me Abbie. I live in a big white house with my mom and dad. I have a cat named Tramp. We are excited at our house because soon we will have a new baby. It will be nice to have a little brother or sister to play with.

Today when I got home from school, I couldn't find my mom. I called for her, but she didn't answer. I went upstairs to look for her. Her bedroom door was closed, and Tramp was lying in the hallway. I heard someone crying in Mom's room. I was kind of scared, but I opened the door anyway. My mom was lying on the bed crying, and her eyes were all red. I hate to see my mom cry. Whenever she does, it makes me want to cry too. I stood in the doorway for a minute because I wasn't sure what to do. Mom finally saw me standing there. She reached out her arms to me, and I ran to her. She hugged me *real* tight.

After she stopped crying, Mom told me that Aunt Jane had just called on the telephone. Grandma was very sick and had been taken to the hospital. Mom said Grandma had had a "stroke."

"What is a stroke?" I asked. Mom told me that a stroke is caused when a blood vessel inside a person's brain gets weak and bursts. Sometimes when people have a stroke, they can't move their arms and legs. Sometimes the arm and leg on only one side won't move. Most times people get better after having a stroke, but sometimes they die. Now I know why Mom is so afraid. I am afraid too.

I know Mom and Dad are worried about Grandma. Mom says that no matter what happens, we should be thankful for our memories. I'm not sure what that means, but it makes me think of the things that make Grandma special to me. I want to ask someone to explain it to me, but I don't want to bother anyone right now. Everyone is so busy worrying about Grandma, making phone calls, and going to the hospital.

* * * * * * * *

I went to the hospital to see Grandma. I thought it would make me feel good, but it didn't. The hospital is big, and it smells funny. Usually, when I visit Grandma it is in her little house, just a few blocks from mine. She bakes me cookies. We watch birds splash in her birdbath. She reads me stories, and we sing songs that Grandma sang when she was my age.

But when I saw Grandma in the hospital, she didn't even act like she knew I was there. She wore a nightgown that didn't belong to her. There were all sorts of tubes running in and out of her. One tube went into her nose, another was connected to a needle in her arm, and I saw wires coming out of the top of her gown. One other tube that came out from under her sheet was connected to a bag hooked to the side of her bed. A nurse stood by her bed, wiping Grandma's forehead with a wet cloth.

I thought if I touched Grandma's hand, she would turn her head and look at me and smile. But when I did touch her hand, it was cold. She didn't open her eyes. I was real mad, because nobody told me she would be like this. I don't want my Grandma to be sick. I want her to be like she was before. I feel afraid.

I walked into the hall, angry and confused. Grandma's nurse followed me. She put her arm around my shoulders. I asked her, "Why does my grandma have to have all that stuff hooked to her?"

"Well, Abbie," the nurse said, "all those tubes and wires are helping your grandma. The tube in her nose helps her breathe. The tube connected to the needle in her arm carries vitamins and minerals because she can't eat. The wires coming out of her gown help us to make sure that her heart is beating evenly. The tube coming out from under the sheet helps her to get rid of urine. We are doing all we can to make your grandma comfortable."

I was glad when the nurse talked to me, but I still felt confused. "Why, does my grandma have someone else's nightgown on? I have stayed all night at her house before, and she never had a nightgown that looked like that."

The nurse said, "Your grandma is wearing the hospital's nightgown because it snaps in the back and on the shoulders. This nightgown makes it easier to check the wires and tubes to make sure they are hooked up correctly."

I was glad I had a chance to talk to the nurse. She helped me understand some of the things that were making me feel confused.

Today on my way home from school, I turned the corner of the street and saw something strange. Lots of cars were parked in front of our house. I saw Mom and Dad's friends walking to our door carrying food. I wasn't sure what was going on, but I knew it had something to do with Grandma. Suddenly, I was really, really scared. I ran home. My heart pounded inside my chest. As I ran through the front yard, I noticed Tramp up on the limb of our big oak tree. He looked frightened too.

As I went through the front door, I saw lots of friends and neighbors in our living room. Sitting on the couch were Mom and Dad. Reverend Jackson, the pastor of our church, was there too.

Mom looked tired and very, very sad. When she saw me, she started to cry. She came across the room to give me a big hug. Suddenly the room got very quiet. I felt everyone looking at me. Mom gently led me by the hand to my room upstairs.

When we got to my room, Mom told me that Grandma had been too sick to get well and that earlier that day she had died. That meant that Grandma and I wouldn't be sharing our cookies and songs anymore. I wouldn't smell her perfume, the stuff that made me think of the lilac bush in our backyard.

When Mom told me this I felt really empty inside, but I didn't cry. I just wanted to be alone. I told this to Mom, and she seemed to understand.

After Mom left, I lay on my back on my bed and looked up at the ceiling for a long time. I tried to pretend that Grandma wasn't really dead, but it didn't work. I didn't think that it would, but I thought if I could forget it for just a few minutes I would feel better. I had all kinds of feelings rushing around

inside me in a ball. I can't say what they all were, but overall I felt really bad. Somehow I felt like Grandma's getting sick was all my fault. I had always tried to be a good girl. I had always tried to be nice and kind to her. Now, I feel mad at her. I just don't know how she could do this to me. It just seems so unfair; I feel really bad.

As I lay on the bed, I looked at the perfume bottles on my dresser. All of a sudden, I couldn't bear the sight of them. I got up from the bed, grabbed a perfume bottle, and smashed it on the floor. As I heard the glass break, it just made me want to smash another, and then another. The strong smell of perfume went all over the house.

Immediately, Mom and Dad and Reverend Jackson came to my room. They all looked very concerned. At first I was afraid they would be mad at me, but then as I looked at them it was like someone had turned on a switch, and I started to cry. I sobbed and sobbed. I didn't want to break things anymore; I just wanted to cry.

Mom and Dad put their arms around me and held me until I was done crying enough to be able to talk. "Why did she have to die?" I asked.

Mom said, "Grandma would never have been like she was before because of the stroke. Her body was just worn out. Besides, Grandma wouldn't have been happy if she wouldn't have been able to go home again. She couldn't do things for herself. She was just too sick to live."

I knew from the things I heard Grandma say lately that she was getting tired. Just a month or so ago I heard Mom tell Aunt Jane that Grandma said she wasn't going to plant so many flowers next year because they were too much work. I just didn't realize that Grandma was not feeling well. I didn't like the idea of Grandma's not being happy, but I didn't like it when she died either. "But Mom," I said, "Grandma hadn't been sick that long. It just isn't fair."

Dad answered, "Everyone has to die sometime. Some people die quickly, while other people are ill for a very long time. I don't think that Grandma's dying is fair either, but much of life seems unfair. It isn't anyone's fault, and even though we get mad at God, God did not make it happen to hurt anyone. Death is part of life."

I asked what would happen to Grandma now. Reverend Jackson told me that some people had taken her body from the hospital to a "funeral home." The people would make her ready so that we could see her one more time. He said they would fix her hair, put some makeup on her so people couldn't tell she had been sick, and put a pretty dress on her. After we saw her for one last time, there would be a funeral, and then Grandma would be buried.

"We must remember, Abbie," Reverend Jackson said, "that what we see at the funeral home and what we bury at the cemetery is only the body your grandma used while she lived here on earth. The part of Grandma that made her who she really was has gone to be with God."

I thought of Grandma sharing her special cookie recipe with God, and even though I felt sad, I had to smile.

* * * * * * *

The next two days before the funeral were kind of confusing to me. I stayed home from school, but it sure wasn't like a vacation. There was lots of food around, and it seemed like we were always eating. For some reason, it made us feel better.

I saw lots of relatives I hadn't seen for a long time. Aunt Jane and her husband were there a lot. Aunt Ellen and Uncle Bill from Chicago stayed at our house. My cousin Sarah, who is only one year older than I, shared my room. Even though we were sad, she and I played a lot. We had fun, and no one seemed to get mad because we laughed and had a good time. My other grandparents, Dad's mom and dad, came from Springfield. It seemed there were lots and lots of people in the house, some I didn't know very well.

The night before the funeral, Mom and Dad said they had a serious question to ask me. This was the night the family would go to the funeral home for the "visitation." That was the time when we would be the first ones to see Grandma's body. Then all our friends would come and be with us. Mom and Dad wanted to know if I wanted to go. They said it was up to me.

I didn't like the thought of seeing Grandma dead. (I hadn't seen anyone dead in my whole life!) But I had been so confused and jumbled up over the last two days that I thought it might be good if I saw her again. Besides, I knew that if they buried her at the cemetery, I wouldn't see her anymore. I thought I'd better see her while I could. I said I would go along with them.

I remember when I was younger and my first kitten died, the one before Tramp. When Dad dug a hole and put my kitten in the ground, it bothered me to see him throw dirt into the grave. Even though my kitten was in a nice shoebox, I was worried about him getting wet and cold. When I told my dad how I felt, he explained that my kitten wouldn't feel anything because he was dead.

When I thought about putting Grandma's body in the ground, it bothered me. Dad told me that Grandma would be in an air-tight steel box called a "casket," and that the casket would be put into a cement box called a "vault," which would be inside her grave. That made me feel better. I decided that by going to the visitation I could maybe find out a few more things about what happens to dead people.

The night of the visitation was cold and clear. I could tell for sure that fall was almost over. Soon the ground would be covered with snow. I could hear the *scratch-scratch* of the leaves as the wind blew them down the street. The moon shone big and bright through the trees.

We walked up the sidewalk toward the funeral home, which looked just like an ordinary house, only bigger. For some reason, I felt a little afraid. Knowing there were dead people inside made it seem spooky. I squeezed my parents' hands real tight.

As we went through the big wooden doors, I looked all around for the dead people, but I couldn't see any. Instead, a friendly looking man came up to us and shook Mom's and Dad's hands. Then he looked down at me and introduced himself as Mr. Pierson, the funeral director. The way he looked at me and talked to me, it was as if I were a grownup too. That made me feel better. He asked us if we were ready to go in and see Grandma. Mom and Dad said yes, and I nodded, even though I wasn't really sure.

Mr. Pierson led us through the main room, which looked like it belonged to a very rich person. Thick carpets stretched from wall to wall. Instead of long white lights like we have at school, a big chandelier hung from the ceiling. I heard soft music coming from somewhere. We walked through a wide doorway, and all of a sudden I saw Grandma. She was at the other end of the room, lying in the casket. My scared feelings went away when I saw Grandma, and I became sad and curious instead.

Grandma lay in the casket, wearing the dress she had always worn to church. I can remember sitting in the front of the church with the Junior Choir and seeing Grandma wearing that dress. The colors of the dress looked pretty with the casket. The color of Grandma's casket reminded me of the pink peonies that grew in her yard in the spring and summer. The inside of the casket was lined with pink material.

Grandma lay in the casket with her hands folded in front of her. She looked as if she were sleeping. All of a sudden I felt like hugging Grandma, but I didn't because she was dead. I did reach out and touch her hand. It was colder than it had been at the hospital. I went over and sat on a chair near the casket. I didn't know what to do, but I felt that I had to be near Grandma as long as I could.

Other people were starting to come in and look at Grandma. Then they would go over to Mom and Aunt Jane and Aunt Ellen

and hug them, and sometimes they cried. I noticed some older women coming in and looking at Grandma. I asked Mom who they were, and she said they were from Grandma's church circle. Some of these ladies cried very, very hard. Most of them had been Grandma's friends for a long, long time. I remember Grandma telling me lots of times about the things she did with her circle ladies. They would make quilts together, take each other shopping, keep each other company, and, now and then, go out to dinner together. When I saw how sad they were, I realized that you don't have to be related to someone to love them.

After a couple of hours, we all went home. I felt really, really tired, but it was hard to go to sleep. I kept thinking about the funeral home and Grandma. Some of my questions had been answered. Now I knew what happens to a person's body when he or she dies. I wondered how life would ever be the same without Grandma. Suddenly I realized that it would never be the same. I decided I would be glad when the funeral was over.

* * * * * * *

Grandma's funeral was this morning. We went to a special room at the funeral home just for the family. I sat between Mom and Dad. Dad's arm was on the back of my chair, and his hand was touching Mom's shoulder. I felt protected and safe. We could see people in the other room, but they couldn't see us. Organ music was playing softly in the background.

After a while, the funeral director and another man wheeled the casket to the front of the room where everyone could see it. The casket was closed, but I knew Grandma was inside. Reverend Jackson came in and sat down at the front of the room. The organ music stopped, and the next thing I heard was the voice of a woman singing a song. I didn't know the song, but the words about being in a garden reminded me of the flowers on Grandma's dress. The thought made me feel sad, and I started to cry. Mom held my hand and squeezed it gently; she started to cry too.

Next, Reverend Jackson stood up and told about when Grandma was born, where she grew up, and when she got married. Some of this I had already heard about from Grandma. Then he told about her family, and I was surprised to hear him read my name.

He read out of the Bible and prayed. He talked about a lot of things. One of the things I liked was when he said that just because someone dies, we don't have to stop loving that person. When he said that, I had the feeling that Grandma, or at least a part of her, would always be inside my heart.

The soloist sang one more song before the funeral director and his helper took Grandma's casket back up the aisle. Someone else took us out the side door, where we got into a big black car with lots of doors. Ahead of us I could see the hearse, which carried Grandma's casket and some of the flowers. Behind us was a long line of cars with their headlights turned on, even though it was daytime. When I asked Dad about this, he explained that it was to show that the cars were part of the funeral. On the way to the cemetery, I saw all of the cars and trucks on the other side of the road pull over and stop. Dad told me this was a sign of respect. It made me feel good to know that Grandma was important to lots and lots of people besides me.

At the cemetery, we stopped next to a big tent with no sides.

Six men, called pallbearers, took Grandma's casket out of the hearse and carried it to the grave. Then we all got out of the cars and walked over to the tent. My parents, aunts, uncles, and grandparents all sat down on some chairs. I stood behind my parents.

Reverend Jackson was there, and he read out of the Bible and prayed. He said again that even though we were putting Grandma's body in the ground, her spirit was with God. It was a sad, sad time for all of us.

Mr. Pierson, the funeral director, took two roses out of the bouquet on the casket. He gave one to my cousin Sarah and one to me. It made me feel important. I also liked it because it made me feel that I was carrying a part of Grandma home with me.

On the way back from the cemetery, Mom said I could put my rose in a book and press it. Then it would last a long time, maybe forever.

We went back to the church and ate dinner. The women in Grandma's circle fixed lots of good food. I noticed that everyone seemed to be talking louder, and there was more laughter than I had heard in many, many days.

It was almost as though everyone felt relieved that the whole thing was finally over. I wondered if it was right for people to be laughing, but then I knew that Grandma wouldn't mind because she also liked to laugh. Suddenly I was very tired, and I wanted to be in my bed.

* * * * * * *

After the funeral, things slowly got back to the way they were before. I went back to school, and my aunts, uncles, grandparents, and my cousin Sarah all went home. We ate Mom's cooking again, and we started to think about the new baby that would soon arrive.

I was excited about the baby, but I was also scared at the thought of Mom's going to the hospital. Grandma died in the hospital, and I didn't want to lose Mom the same way. As the days went on, I got more scared. I spent more and more time in my room. One day Mom asked me why I was being so quiet. I told her I was afraid she was going to die when she went to the hospital. She hugged me and told me that not everyone who goes to the hospital dies, especially if they are going just to have a baby. Most people who go to the hospital get well and come home. That made me feel lots better.

This morning when I came downstairs for breakfast, I was surprised to see our neighbor, Mrs. Wadsworth, in the kitchen. She gave me a big smile and a hug and told me that she had a surprise for me. Late in the night Dad had taken Mom to the hospital. It was time for the baby. Dad would be calling soon to tell us what was happening.

Mrs. Wadsworth fixed me scrambled eggs, toast, and hot cocoa. As I was finishing the last of my cocoa, the phone rang. Mrs. Wadsworth told me to answer it because it was probably for me. Sure enough, when I said hello, Dad said that the baby had been born. It was a girl! I almost dropped the phone because I was so excited. But all of a sudden I felt a hard knot in my tummy because I thought of Mom. Before I could ask Dad about her, he said Mom was doing fine! I asked him how soon I could see Mom and the baby, and he said right after school. I was so excited all day that I could hardly concentrate. The day seemed to drag by. I didn't think 3:15 would ever come.

When I finally got out of school, Dad was waiting for me in the car. We drove to the hospital. As I walked down the halls this time, it seemed like a much friendlier place. The nurses smiled at us as we walked up to the desk. One of the nurses took us to a big window where we could see the babies. The nurse inside went over to a row of babies, lifted one up, and brought it over to us.

"Say hello to your new little sister," said Dad. I looked at her; she was fast asleep. She had lots of black hair and a real red face. To me, she was beautiful.

"What's her name?" I asked. Dad said that he and Mom wanted to know if I had a favorite name in mind. I said I had always liked the name "Emily." Dad said he and Mom would talk it over and decide later.

That night when I went to bed, all I could think about was my baby sister. I thought about all the fun things we could do as she grew up. It was going to be nice having someone to share with. When Emily comes home, our lives will be so busy!

Even though I love Emily and like to spend lots of time with her, sometimes I like to be by myself. When I am, I take quiet walks. I like to walk by the house where Grandma lived. Some other people bought it and live there now, but I'll always think of it as Grandma's. It reminds me that, even though Grandma died, I can still love her, and she loves me back. And that makes me very happy.

When Emily is old enough to understand, I want to tell her all about Grandma. That way, Emily can love her too.

THE END

An Afterword—Hey Kids!

Has someone you really loved ever died? If you've gone through what Abbie did in this story, you know that there are times when you felt that you were all alone. There was nobody to talk to, and you had a lot of questions you really needed answers for.

There are lots of people around you who will be glad to talk to you about what happens when someone dies. Try your parents first. It's always good to go to them when you're wondering about stuff, and most of the time they're glad to help. Press them for answers. Ask the questions that are really on your mind.

If they are not able to answer your questions or you'd like another opinion, talk with your minister, a school counselor, a teacher, your family doctor, or any other adult whom you consider to be a good friend. If all else fails, write to us, and we'll do our best to answer your questions by return mail. Send your questions to:

Roger F. Miller
Hollie J. Harbaugh
c/o Grandma Book
Central Christian Church
Jefferson, Iowa 50129

Believe us, if you get your questions answered—and the sooner the better—things won't seem quite so strange when the time comes to go through hard times. The important thing is to talk about your feelings, and if you feel like crying, go ahead and do it.

Roger and Hollie